P9-CFC-203

FOUR in ALL

For Cecilia, Sophia, Ada,
Olivia, Kai, ...

Copyright © 2001 by Nina Payne
Illustrations copyright © 2001 by Adam S. Payne
Printed in China
All rights reserved
CIP data available
First edition

Nina Payne

Four in All

Illustrated by Adam Payne

Front Street
Asheville, North Carolina

eyes ears nose mouth

oats wheat corn rye

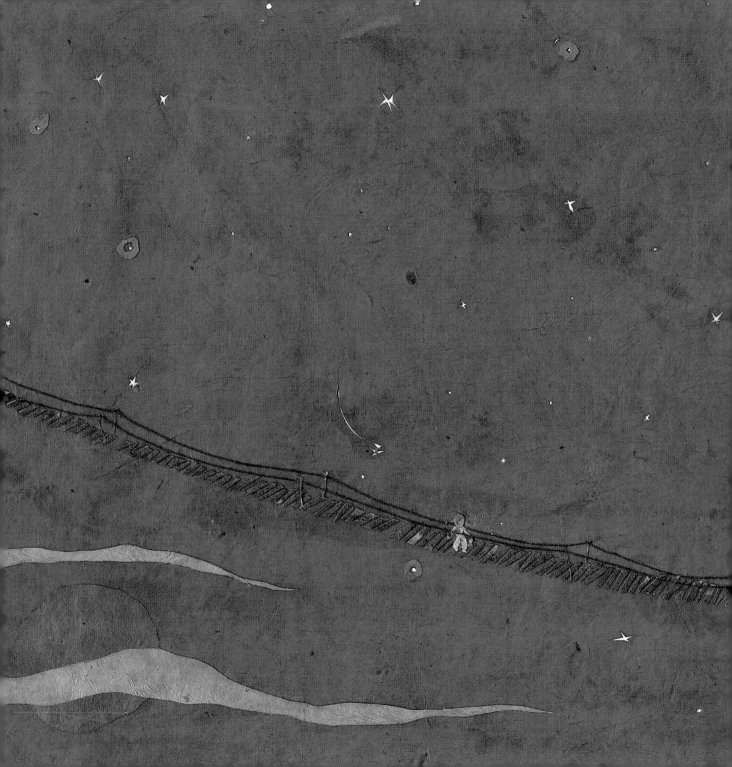

sun moon stars sky

floor table chair bed

one two three four

roof window chimney door

bird fish bear snake

ocean river puddle lake

fork plate knife spoon

morning evening midnight noon

mother father son daughter

eyes ears nose mouth
east west north south

oats wheat corn rye
sun moon stars sky

floor table chair bed
yellow green blue red

one two three four
roof window chimney door

bird fish bear snake
ocean river puddle lake

fork plate knife spoon
morning evening midnight noon

earth air fire water
mother father son daughter